WEST VIRGINIA

Hello U.S.A.

WEST VIRGINIA

Domenica Di Piazza

Lerner Publications Company

Cover photograph courtesy of Stephen J. Shaluta, Jr., West Virginia Division of Tourism and Parks.

The glossary on page 69 gives definitions of words shown in **bold type** in the text.

LIBRARY OF CONGRESS
CATALOGING-IN-PUBLICATION DATA
Di Piazza, Domenica.
  West Virginia / Domenica Di Piazza.
    p.   cm. — (Hello U.S.A.)
  Includes index.
  ISBN 0-8225-2745-6 (lib. bdg.)
    1. West Virginia—Juvenile literature. [1. West Virginia.] I. Title. II. Series.
F241.3.D52 1995
917.54—dc20   93-46906
                                    CIP
                                     AC

Manufactured in the United States of America

1 2 3 4 5 6 – I/JR – 00 99 98 97 96 95

This book is printed on acid-free, recyclable paper.

CONTENTS

White-water rafters pass under the New River Gorge Bridge.

Did You Know . . . ?

❑ The New River Gorge Bridge near Fayetteville, West Virginia, is the second highest bridge in the United States. The top of this steel arch bridge stands almost 900 feet (274 meters) above the New River.

❑ Scientists from all over the world come to the National Radio Astronomy Observatory in Green Bank, West Virginia, to study outer space using the observatory's giant radio telescopes.

❑ The nation's first Mother's Day was celebrated in Grafton, West Virginia, on May 10, 1908. Just a few months later, on July 5, resi-

dents of Fairmont, West Virginia, marked the first Father's Day.

☐ Factories in Parkersburg, West Virginia, manufacture most of the glass marbles produced in the United States.

☐ In 1912 farmers in central West Virginia became the first in the nation to raise Golden Delicious apples. Each fall the town of Clay, West Virginia, hosts the Golden Delicious Festival to celebrate this popular fruit.

A Trip Around the State

If you're looking for flat land in West Virginia, chances are you won't have much luck. Mountains and steep hills rise from one end of the state to the other. For this reason, West Virginia is known as the Mountain State, and residents call themselves Mountaineers.

West Virginia's rugged landscape is part of a large mountain system called the Appalachians. Millions of years ago, the area that is now West Virginia was almost flat. But over time, huge layers of rock folded and lifted upward to form the Appalachian Mountains. Rain, wind, and rushing rivers carved out deep valleys.

Boulders *(left)* jut from the ground in the Monongahela National Forest in eastern West Virginia. This forest includes almost one million acres (405,000 hectares) of the Allegheny Mountains *(below),* which are part of the Appalachian system.

9

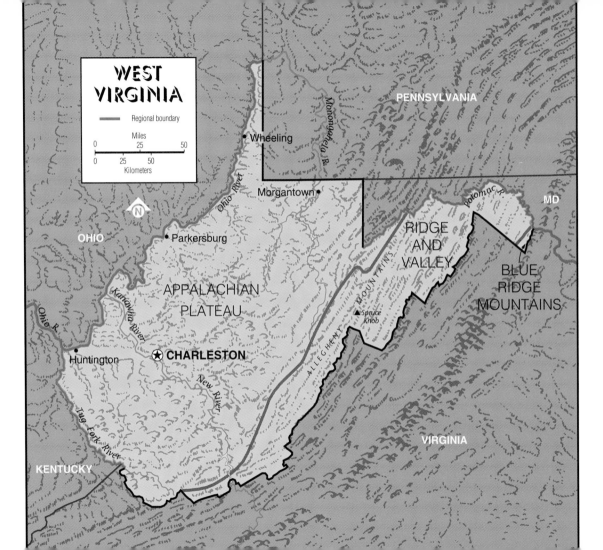

WEST VIRGINIA

Regional boundary

Miles
0   25   50

0   25   50
Kilometers

N

PENNSYLVANIA

Monongahela R.

Wheeling

Ohio River

Morgantown

MD

Potomac R.

OHIO

Parkersburg

RIDGE
AND
VALLEY

BLUE
RIDGE
MOUNTAINS

Kanawha River

APPALACHIAN
PLATEAU

ALLEGHENY   MOUNTAINS

▲ Spruce
Knob

Ohio R.

★ CHARLESTON

Huntington

New River

VIRGINIA

Tug Fork River

KENTUCKY

West Virginia is easy to identify on a map because it is the only state in the country with two panhandles. Known as the Eastern and the Northern panhandles, these areas of land are shaped something like the handles on frying pans. Mountaineers sometimes joke that their state is a great place, considering the shape it's in.

A Mid-Atlantic state, West Virginia shares its borders with five other states. Across the Ohio River, to the west, lies Ohio. To the southwest, across the Tug Fork River, is Kentucky. Mountain peaks separate West Virginia from Virginia in the east. Maryland lies to the northeast, and Pennsylvania borders the northwest.

West Virginia has three regions—

Colorful leaves brighten West Virginia's landscape in fall.

the Blue Ridge Mountains, the Ridge and Valley, and the Appalachian Plateau. These regions are part of the Appalachian system, which covers the entire state.

11

The Blue Ridge Mountains stretch across the Eastern Panhandle.

The Blue Ridge Mountains rise in the northeastern corner of West Virginia. When seen from far away, the forested slopes of this range appear blue—the color for which the mountains are named. Farmers raise fruit trees in the region's river valleys.

The Ridge and Valley runs the length of West Virginia's eastern border. Extending over much of the region are the Allegheny Mountains, where the state's highest peak—Spruce Knob—rises. Rivers wind through narrow valleys that separate these tree-covered ridges.

The Appalachian Plateau covers the rest of West Virginia. Most of the state's biggest cities are located in the river valleys of the **plateau,** an area of high land. Rich deposits of minerals such as coal, petroleum, natural gas, and salt lie underground in this region.

Oak trees are common in the forests of the Alleghenies *(above)*. An early frost *(inset)* covers the deep red leaves of an oak.

13

For more than 100 years, West Virginians have relied on rivers for shipping coal and other minerals to market. The Mountaineers built cities near these busy water highways. Huntington and Wheeling, two of the state's largest cities, grew along the banks of the Ohio River. Charleston, the state capital, lies along the Kanawha River. Other important waterways in the state include the Monongahela, the Potomac, and the New rivers.

West Virginia receives about 50 inches (127 centimeters) of **precipitation** (rain, sleet, and snow) every year. Most of the snow falls in the mountains, where up to 100

Tugboats line the banks of the Kanawha River in downtown Charleston.

Snow coats trees in a West Virginia forest.

inches (254 cm) may blanket the highest peaks in winter. Less than 20 inches (51 cm) of snow falls in the southwest.

Winters in West Virginia are coldest high up in the mountains. Midwinter temperatures on the slopes average about 22° F (−6° C), while temperatures in the valleys stay several degrees warmer. In summer, people living high in the mountains enjoy cooler weather than residents of cities such as Charleston. The average summer temperature in this river town is about 87° F (31° C).

The hepatica is one of the first flowers to bloom every spring in West Virginia.

Anglers find plenty of bass, trout, and walleye in West Virginia's rivers and streams. Foxes, opossums, and raccoons make their homes in the state's forests. Bears, deer, and beavers outnumber people in some areas!

West Virginia's forests stretch across most of the state. Evergreen trees, such as white pine, red spruce, and hemlock, grow on mountainsides and in river valleys. Hardwoods include maple, cherry, oak, and tulip trees. Dogwood, redbud, hawthorn, and other flowering trees open their buds each spring in the state's river valleys.

Early summer is a great time to see the colorful blossoms of West Virginia's state flower, the rhododendron. Asters and black-eyed Susans bloom into the fall. And Mountaineers know it's spring again when dainty hepatica flowers begin to bud.

In a West Virginia forest
(left), **a bear cub** *(inset)*
explores a hollow log
while a fawn *(above)*
takes a nap.

17

Mammoths looked something like elephants. From studying mammoth bones, scientists know that some of the animals stood more than 14 feet (4.2 meters) tall and had tusks 13 feet (3.9 m) long.

West Virginia's Story

The first people in North America were hunters. Scientists believe that these people came from Asia at least 15,000 years ago by walking across a land bridge that once connected these two continents. Over thousands of years, descendants of the early hunters made their way to what is now West Virginia.

Traveling in small groups, the hunters moved from place to place and used spears to kill mammoths and other large prey. When these huge animals became extinct around 8,000 B.C., the people survived by fishing, hunting smaller game such as deer, and gathering nuts and berries.

Descendants of the hunters and gatherers began building permanent villages along the Ohio River around 1000 B.C. Villagers raised pumpkins and sunflowers for food and tobacco to smoke during special ceremonies. Round homes built from poles, mud, and bark provided shelter for families.

Chiefs and priests lived on top of huge earthen mounds. When they died, these leaders were buried in log tombs covered with many piles of dirt. Because they constructed so many giant earthworks, these people came to be known as mound builders.

Although most of the mounds in what is now West Virginia were built along the Ohio and Kanawha rivers, other mounds were scattered across the region. But by about A.D. 1500, the mound builders had abandoned their villages. No one knows exactly what happened, but experts think that warfare, disease, or lack of rain may have forced the mound builders to leave their homes.

The largest of its kind in the United States, the Grave Creek Mound near Moundsville, West Virginia, contains about 60,000 tons (54,432 metric tons) of dirt.

At about the same time, far across the Atlantic Ocean, Great Britain and other European countries imagined North America to be a land of many riches. Hoping to gain some of this wealth, these countries began to set up **colonies,** or settlements, in America.

In 1607 three boats carrying British settlers landed at the mouth of the James River in the Virginia Colony. Recently founded by Great Britain, the colony stretched between what are now Pennsylvania and South Carolina. The colony's western boundaries, however, had not been established.

Traders soon began to explore the Virginia Colony in search of valuable fur-bearing animals such as beavers. In 1671 an expedition led by Thomas Batts and Robert Fallam crossed the Alleghenies into what is now eastern West Virginia. There, they claimed the New River valley for Great Britain.

Alexander Spotswood crossed the Blue Ridge Mountains into what is now West Virginia in 1716. He was one of the state's earliest British explorers.

Indians in what is now West Virginia hunted game animals by trapping the prey in rings of fire.

Farther west, French fur traders were exploring the Ohio River valley, hoping to expand their fur-trading business in North America. The French and the British met Native Americans from many different nations (or tribes) in what is now West Virginia. These groups, possibly descended from the early mound builders, included the Cherokee, Shawnee, Delaware, Mingo, and Iroquois Indians.

Although the Indians did not make permanent homes in what is now West Virginia, they used the area as a hunting ground. Indians supplied the Europeans with furs and received kettles, beads, and hatchets in exchange. Traders transported the furs to European countries, where the pelts sold for very high prices.

As the British expanded their fur trade west toward the Ohio River, German and Scotch-Irish farmers came to what is now West Virginia. Over time these pioneers claimed more and more territory. Settlers and Native Americans disagreed about who had rights to the land, and fighting sometimes broke out.

Meanwhile the British and the French were arguing over the Ohio River valley. The British felt that Batts and Fallam had claimed the land in 1671. But the French believed that the valley belonged to France, since French adventurers had explored the region as well.

The French tried to keep control of the Ohio River valley by burying lead plates inscribed with their claim to the land.

Many of West Virginia's cities developed around forts, such as Fort Fincastle (later Fort Henry) near Wheeling. Settlers fled to the forts for protection during attacks and battles.

By 1754 the disagreement had led to the French and Indian War. Some of the bloodiest battles of this conflict were fought in what is now West Virginia. The French encouraged their Indian allies to attack British pioneers in the area. As a result, few new settlers came to the region.

After winning the war in 1763, Great Britain gained control of almost all the land between the Atlantic Ocean and the Mississippi River. Five years later, the British signed **treaties,** or agreements, with the Cherokee and the Iroquois nations. In exchange for a payment, these Indian nations gave up their claim to most of their land in what is now West Virginia. After this, settlers came to the region by the thousands.

Lord Dunmore's War

After the French and Indian War, thousands of pioneers made their way to what is now West Virginia. Many of these settlers built homes in the Ohio River valley, on land that Indian nations had not given up. As a result, settlers and Indians often clashed violently.

In an attack in April 1774, settlers killed the family of a Mingo chief named Logan. Logan, who had been friendly to white people for many years, felt betrayed and took up arms. He was joined by the Shawnee leader Cornstalk and his forces. Under Cornstalk, Indian troops battled the army of Lord Dunmore, the governor of the Virginia Colony. The conflict, known as Lord Dunmore's War, ended when Lord Dunmore defeated the Indians at the Battle of Point Pleasant that fall.

Logan, who had been asked to come to the peace negotiations, chose not to attend. Instead he sent a letter expressing his thoughts about the events that had led to the war. In the famous letter, Logan wrote that because his entire family had been murdered, "There runs not a drop of my blood in the veins of any living creature. This called upon me for revenge. I have sought it. . . . I rejoice at the beams of peace. . . . [But] who is there to mourn for Logan? Not one."

Chief Logan

Lord Dunmore

George Washington, a Virginian who had led British troops during the French and Indian War, owned land in what is now West Virginia. But he was soon asked to lead troops in another war—the American War of Independence.

In this war, which started in 1775, British colonists in North America fought to win their independence from Great Britain. Many settlers from what is now West Virginia fought in the colonial army. Others sewed clothing and grew crops to help feed colonial soldiers.

The colonists finally defeated the British in 1783 and formed a new country—the United States of America. Six years later, George Washington became the new nation's first president. Virginia, which included what is now West Virginia, became one of the first states. At the time, few people lived in western Virginia. But as settlers built new roads across the Allegheny Mountains, more people came to the region.

Many of the newcomers were farmers. Others were attracted by salt-mining jobs near Charleston in the Kanawha River valley. Laborers found jobs mining coal to fuel the furnaces where salt was produced. Workers crafted wooden barrels for storing the salt or built boats to ship the salt to market. By 1815 salt furnaces in the Charleston area were manufacturing about 3,000 bushels of salt every day.

Oil was discovered in West Virginia by miners digging for salt. With little use for the oil, miners threw it into nearby waterways. At one time, the Kanawha River *(above)* was so full of oil that it became known as Old Greasy.

Carriage rides along West Virginia's bumpy roads were so rough that the vehicles were known as "shake-guts."

Agricultural industries were also booming. Blacksmiths fashioned plows and other farm equipment from iron bars made by the region's iron workers. Factories in growing cities such as Wheeling made clothing out of sheep's wool from the Northern Panhandle.

From Wheeling, steamboats loaded with cattle, flour, glass, and wool headed to towns along the Ohio and Mississippi rivers. After the Baltimore & Ohio Railroad laid tracks to Wheeling in 1852, trains began transporting goods to cities on the eastern side of the Appalachians.

At this time, railroads and trade were linking communities across the country. But many Americans were still divided over the issue of slavery. In Northern states, slavery was illegal. But many farmers in Virginia and other Southern states used slaves to work huge farms called **plantations**.

Although the North pressured the South to end slavery, Southern planters were determined to keep slaves. In 1860 Southern states formed the Confederate States of America (the Confederacy), an independent country where slavery remained legal.

Virginians were split over whether to join the new country. Most of the state's slaves worked on tobacco plantations east of the Alleghenies. To the west, the land was too mountainous for large farms. Most farmers did not own slaves.

John Brown's Raid

John Brown spent most of his life helping black people escape slavery. In the 1850s, he planned to set up a community of African Americans in the Appalachians in what is now West Virginia. From there, Brown could lead attacks against slaveholders, which he hoped would lead to a massive slave rebellion. To do this, Brown needed weapons and ammunition.

On the night of October 16, 1859, Brown and a small army of supporters seized a warehouse in Harpers Ferry, where the U.S. government stored weapons. Word of the raid spread, and U.S. marines captured and arrested the group. Although Brown was tried for treason and hanged, his dream of ending slavery came true soon after his death.

In memory of John Brown, Union soldiers marching to battle sang, "John Brown's body lies a-moldering in the grave, His soul goes marching on."

After the Civil War broke out between the North and the South in 1861, Virginia voted to join the Confederacy. But most people in northwestern Virginia supported the North (the Union). In 1862 they approved a **constitution** (a set of written laws) for a new state to be called West Virginia. On June 20, 1863, the U.S. government admitted West Virginia as the 35th state.

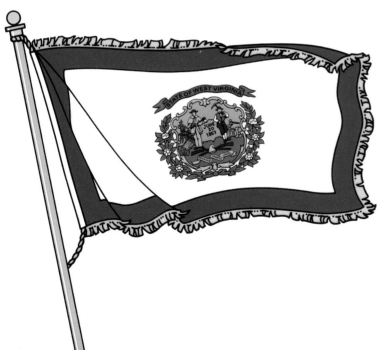

The date West Virginia joined the Union appears on the coat of arms in the center of the state's flag. Beneath the date is West Virginia's motto— *Montani Semper Liberi* (Mountaineers Are Always Free).

Confederate soldiers in West Virginia raided towns for food supplies, including salt and hogs.

Although most soldiers in West Virginia fought for the Union, at least 8,000 men joined the army of the Confederacy. Some families were bitterly split, with fathers and sons fighting on opposite sides.

In the early part of the war, Union troops defeated the Confederates in West Virginia and kept control of the state. But some Confederate soldiers fought back. They burned bridges and villages, destroyed homes, and stole salt, crops, and livestock. In 1865, after four long years of conflict, the Union won the war.

Several new railroad companies built tracks across West Virginia after the Civil War. The tracks led into remote forests and opened up areas rich in coal and oil. Towns sprang up almost overnight along the tracks or wherever a new mine opened.

Mining and logging industries boomed in West Virginia in the late 1800s. By 1899 workers at nearly 1,000 sawmills across the state were producing lumber for wood products such as boats, houses, and railroad ties. Each year wells were pumping more than 10 million barrels of oil, and coal miners were digging up more than 18 million tons (16 million metric tons) of coal.

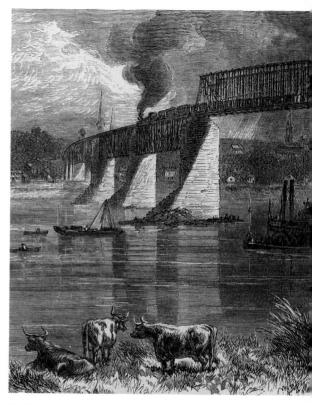

Railroads linked West Virginia's towns, transporting people and goods faster than carriages or steamships could.

In the early 1900s, more coal miners died on the job in West Virginia than in any other coal-mining state in the country.

As industries grew, so did West Virginia's population, which rose to almost one million people in 1900. Some of the new residents were Italian, Polish, Hungarian, Austrian, and Russian **immigrants,** who had come to the United States hoping for a better life. Many of these newcomers found jobs in West Virginia's coal mines.

Miners worked deep under the ground and faced many dangers on the job. Coal dust that collected in the mines caused a deadly disease called black lung. Poisonous gases built up in the mines and often exploded, killing hundreds of miners.

In the early 1900s, many of West Virginia's coal miners joined a

Union organizer Mary ("Mother") Jones came to West Virginia in the early 1900s to help coal miners form unions and fight for their rights.

union (workers' organization) called the United Mine Workers of America (UMWA). The union organized strikes among its members, who refused to work unless their employers provided safer working conditions and better pay.

Most mining companies were angered by the strikes and forced new employees to sign papers agreeing not to join the union. The companies also hired guards to prevent union organizers from coming to talk to miners. The miners who did join the UMWA were sometimes beaten up by company guards or locked out of their homes, which were usually owned by the coal mining companies.

During the Great Depression, the U.S. government put many of West Virginia's jobless people *(above)* back to work. About 60,000 people built or repaired roads, many of which were in poor condition *(right)*.

Despite the strikes, coal companies made few changes. Many miners gave up hope and left the UMWA. In 1921, 42,000 miners belonged to the union, but by 1929 the number had dropped to only 1,000.

That same year marked the beginning of the Great Depression. Banks failed, businesses closed, and millions of workers lost their jobs. In West Virginia, the number of people without jobs was higher than in many other states.

To help West Virginia, the U.S. government created new jobs. Workers were hired to build roads and clear hiking paths through the state's forests.

New laws also improved working conditions. Workdays were shortened to eight hours. Companies had to pay workers a minimum wage, and they could no longer prevent their workers from joining unions. As a result, more West Virginian coal miners than ever before joined the UMWA.

West Virginia's mines thrived during World War II (1939–1945), when coal was needed to fuel factory furnaces and freight trains. Workers in the state produced steel, ships, and weapons. Salt was used to manufacture plastic, rubber, and other products useful during wartime.

After the war, demand for coal dropped as oil and natural gas became the nation's major sources of energy. At the same time, West Virginia's mines began to use machines that dug up more coal than miners could. Less coal and fewer miners were needed, and many workers lost their jobs. Thousands left the state in the 1950s and 1960s to look for work elsewhere.

To help the state's economy, the

During World War II, the world's largest synthetic rubber factory was built in Institute, West Virginia.

An explosion in 1968 at a coal mine in West Virginia led to new safety laws.

U.S. government created a program in 1965 to retrain workers in West Virginia and in other Appalachian states. Jobless coal miners learned the skills needed for building roads, for restoring forestland, and for other occupations.

In the 1970s, a nationwide shortage of oil created a strong demand for West Virginia's coal. New mining jobs and work in the state's growing chemical, metal, and glass industries attracted people to the state and helped West Virginia's population grow. By 1980 the Mountain State had more than 1.9 million residents.

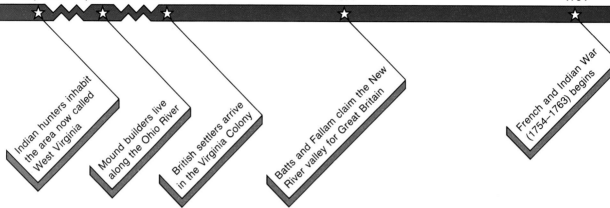

| 13,000 B.C. | 1,000 B.C. | A.D. 1607 | 1671 | 1754 |

Indian hunters inhabit the area now called West Virginia

Mound builders live along the Ohio River

British settlers arrive in the Virginia Colony

Batts and Fallam claim the New River valley for Great Britain

French and Indian War (1754–1763) begins

When the oil shortage ended in the 1980s, mines in West Virginia closed down and coal miners again lost their jobs. By 1984 more people were out of work in West Virginia than anywhere else in the country. By 1990 West Virginia's population had dropped to 1.7 million residents.

West Virginians are looking for ways to make their economy less dependent on coal. By building better roads, the state has improved transportation. This has attracted some new industries, including tourism, to West Virginia. Thousands of workers earn a living helping tourists discover and enjoy the natural beauty and history of the Mountain State, a place West Virginians are proud to call home.

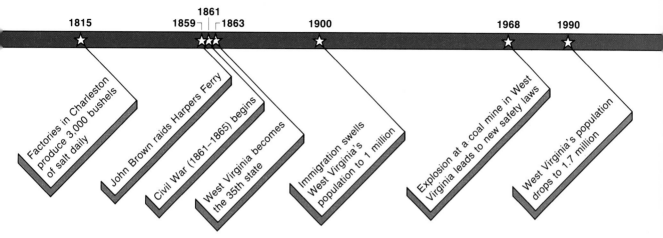

1815
Factories in Charleston produce 3,000 bushels of salt daily

1859
John Brown raids Harpers Ferry

1861
Civil War (1861–1865) begins

1863
West Virginia becomes the 35th state

1900
Immigration swells West Virginia's population to 1 million

1968
Explosion at a coal mine in West Virginia leads to new safety laws

1990
West Virginia's population drops to 1.7 million

The National Radio Astronomy Observatory in Green Bank, West Virginia—home to some of the largest radio telescopes in the world—is one of the state's most popular tourist attractions.

Rock climbers find plenty of cliff-hanging challenges in West Virginia.

Living and Working in West Virginia

Echo and Falling Rock. Droop and Hominy Falls. Big Chimney and Tornado. About two-thirds of West Virginia's 1.7 million residents live in these and other small towns and rural areas across the state. Cities such as Charleston (the state capital), Huntington, Wheeling, Parkersburg, and Morgantown are home to the rest of the Mountain State's population.

Small towns dot the landscape throughout West Virginia.

Most Mountaineers—96 percent—trace their ancestry to immigrants from European countries such as Germany, Ireland, and Italy. African Americans make up about 3 percent of the population, while Native Americans, Asian Americans, and Latinos together number less than 1 percent of the state's residents.

In the 1800s, most West Virginians made a living on a family farm. Nowadays only 4 percent of all working West Virginians have jobs in agriculture. Most farms in the Mountain State are small and located in river valleys. Farmers raise beef and dairy cattle, chickens, and turkeys. West Virginia's crops include hay, corn, and tobacco. Apples and peaches are grown in the eastern part of the state.

Some tobacco farmers in West Virginia use mules to pull plows.

Most of West Virginia's beef and dairy cattle *(left)* are raised in the southeastern part of the state. Throughout the state, abundant forests of oak, cherry, and other hardwood trees make West Virginia a leader in harvesting timber *(above)*.

Salt is still important to West Virginia's mining economy. But coal makes more money for the state than any other mineral. In fact, rich deposits of coal lie under half of West Virginia's land. About 5 percent of the state's workers have mining jobs, digging coal and pumping natural gas and oil. Other miners scoop up sand for making

glass and concrete. Limestone is crushed and used in building roads.

More than 80,000 workers—or 14 percent of all jobholders in West Virginia—earn a living from manufacturing. Steel mills in the state use iron ore from the Midwest to make sheets of steel and giant beams for construction.

Other products are made from West Virginia's natural resources. Chemical plants along the Ohio and Kanawha rivers use local supplies of salt, coal, natural gas, and oil to make dyes, paints, plastics, rubber, soaps, and other chemical products.

Only Wyoming and Kentucky produce more coal (inset) than West Virginia. The state's stone, gravel, sand, and limestone are used in building roads, such as the highway (left) that crosses the New River Gorge Bridge.

The guides who help rafters tackle West Virginia's rushing waterways are among the state's many service workers.

West Virginia is famous for its pottery and glassware. Workers at pottery plants mold clay into dishes, bricks, and tiles. Using local sand, the state's glassware factories turn out dinner glasses, bottles, stained glass, and large sheets of glass.

Most workers in West Virginia have service jobs helping people and businesses. Service workers include the state's governor as well as doctors, lawyers, and teachers. Even the hot-dog vendors working at a Mountaineers football game at West Virginia University have service jobs.

The salesclerks who sell West Virginia's glassware and chemical products are also part of the service workforce. So are the people

Bicyclists tour West Virginia's scenic countryside.

who load the Mountain State's coal and lumber onto barges and trains headed for market. Altogether, 73 percent of working West Virginians have service jobs.

Service workers also help the millions of tourists who come to West Virginia each year. Many vis-itors enjoy the thrill of rafting down the New and the Gauley rivers, which are known for their white-water rapids. Cyclists tour the Greenbrier River Trail, an old railroad bed that passes through numerous small towns, over 35 bridges, and through two tunnels.

Campers head for West Virginia's many parks and forests, where they can also hike, ski, or ride horses and mountain bikes. Rock climbers can test their skills on the 900-foot (274-m) cliff at Seneca Rocks. Each winter, ski resorts attract downhill skiers, who zoom down the state's snow-covered Appalachian peaks.

The people of the Appalachian Mountains are known for their unique culture. At the Augusta Heritage Center in Elkins, visitors can learn to play and sing traditional bluegrass tunes. Dancers can attend classes on Appalachian clogging, while other students discover how to weave baskets and sew quilts.

A hiker *(above)* **inspects a tree hit by lightning. Country music attracts crowds** *(facing page, left)* **to Wheeling. In Clarksburg a woman in costume** *(facing page, right)* **enjoys the Italian Heritage Festival.**

Each September in Clarksburg, the popular West Virginia Italian Heritage Festival offers lively entertainment by singers, dancers, and puppeteers dressed in colorful costumes. Brass bands and yodeling are part of the fun at Weston's Oktoberfest, a celebration of the state's Swiss, Austrian, and German heritage.

Many people enjoy the Mountain State's music festivals. Every July thousands of people jam the streets of Wheeling on their way to hear famous country-music singers at Jamboree in the Hills. Mountaineers perform gospel tunes at the Vandalia Gathering in Charleston. And no trip to West Virginia is complete without tapping your toes at one of the state's many bluegrass festivals.

51

West Virginia offers many opportunities to discover the state's history. Visitors to the Grave Creek Mound in Moundsville can learn about the mound-building Indians who once lived in the area. The pioneer cabin at Charleston's Cultural Center shows what daily life was like for the state's early settlers. A visit to the John Brown Museum in Harpers Ferry is a good way to learn about the events that led to the Civil War.

At the Beckley Exhibition Coal Mine, groups go underground to see how miners dug for coal in the late 1800s. Those who prefer to travel back in time above the ground can learn more about West Virginia's history aboard the Cass Scenic Railroad.

This old-fashioned steam-powered train takes passengers up the steep slopes of Bald Knob Mountain, the second highest point in the state. From here, viewers can look out over the rugged landscape and feel a bit of Mountaineer pride themselves.

Bridges *(left)* along the Cass Scenic Railroad add to the fun of the train ride. In the early 1900s, steam-powered trains *(above)* on this railroad carried timber from the state's forests to its sawmills.

Some Mountaineers illegally dispose of trash in places that aren't meant for garbage.

Protecting the Environment

Garbage. In 1990 West Virginians threw out about 1.4 million tons (1.3 million metric tons) of household trash and other solid waste. That's about 3,900 tons (3,500 metric tons) of garbage every day, or more than 4 pounds (1.8 kilograms) per person per day.

More than 90 percent of West Virginia's garbage is buried in **landfills**—giant pits dug in the earth for burying solid waste. In addition, some of the state's trash is dropped unlawfully on the side of the road and at thousands of other illegal dumps across the state.

Huge bulldozers pack trash in landfills.

Some of New York City's garbage is sent to West Virginia to be buried.

Along with its own garbage, the Mountain State also buries solid waste from nearby states such as Pennsylvania, New York, and New Jersey. These states, which have high populations and overflowing landfills, pay West Virginia to dispose of extra garbage. In 1990, for example, West Virginia buried almost 750,000 tons (680,400 metric tons) of garbage from outside the Mountain State.

Burying other people's garbage is a big business that earns many states, including West Virginia, millions of dollars each year. But the garbage in these states is piling up quickly too.

In the early 1990s, West Virginians realized that they would soon be over their heads in garbage if something did not change. The amount of out-of-state garbage was increasing, and lines of garbage trucks waiting to dump their loads at landfills were getting longer and longer. The number of garbage truck accidents and spills was also rising.

Some Mountaineers have put up signs to show concern about garbage in their state.

Garbage Soup

The garbage placed in landfills eventually begins to decompose, or rot, turning into a soupy liquid called **leachate.** Rainwater filters down through the rotting trash and mixes with the leachate. This garbage soup, which carries germs and poisonous chemicals, soaks into the soil beneath the landfill and eventually pollutes the **groundwater.** This valuable source of drinking water for homes and businesses can then become unsafe to use.

To prevent leachate from reaching the groundwater, West Virginia requires workers to line new landfills with layers of heavy clay soil or thick plastic. Many landfills are also built with special drainage layers that collect the leachate, which is then piped to nearby sewage plants to be treated.

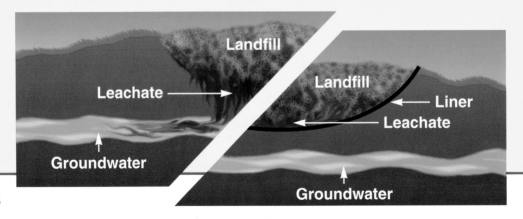

Landfills that were expected to fill up in 20 years were overflowing after only 7 years. No laws existed to limit the amount of garbage that could be buried in the state. As a result, West Virginia was quickly using up land and spending a lot of money to build new landfills.

To keep garbage under control, West Virginia passed a solid waste law in 1991. This law limits the amount of in-state and out-of-state garbage that can be dumped at each landfill to 30,000 tons (27,216 metric tons) per month. West Virginia also established a new recycling program to help residents cut down on the amount of garbage they throw out.

Young Mountaineers recycle newspapers.

Through the recycling program, West Virginians are aiming to generate only half as much garbage per person in the year 2010 as they did in 1991. By reducing the amount of garbage, West Virginia's leaders hope to slow down the rate at which landfills fill up. If they succeed, the state won't have to keep building additional landfills.

West Virginians are participating in the plan to reduce garbage in many ways. Residents place glass, newspapers, plastics, and other recyclable materials at the curb for monthly pickup. Government offices are now buying and using recycled paper and other recycled products. Many of the state's newspaper publishers are using recycled newsprint in their newpapers. And West Virginia's schools are teaching students about solid waste and recycling.

So far the efforts have paid off. By the end of 1993, West Virginia had about 26,500 tons (24,041 metric tons) less garbage to bury than it had in 1992. The state expects to bury even less garbage in the near future. West Virginians want to work together to make sure the Mountain State doesn't become the Garbage State.

Many West Virginians pick up trash along roads and highways as part of the state's Adopt-a-Highway program.

West Virginia's Famous People

Bricktop (1894–1984) was an entertainer and nightclub owner whose nickname came from her flaming red hair and freckles. Born Ada Smith in Alderson, West Virginia, she moved to Paris and opened Bricktop's in the 1920s. The famous club featured American music and drew many well-known patrons.

Joanne Dru (born 1923) was a leading actress in many Western film classics, such as *Red River, Wagonmaster,* and *She Wore a Yellow Ribbon.* Dru is from Logan, West Virginia.

Don Knotts (born 1924) is a comic actor known for his role as the deputy on "The Andy Griffith Show," a popular television program of the 1960s. A native of Morgantown, West Virginia, Knotts also starred in several movie comedies.

◀ JOANNE DRU

DON ▶ KNOTTS

Peter Marshall (born 1930) won five Emmy Awards as the host of "The Hollywood Squares." Starting in 1966, he questioned famous guests in more than 5,000 editions of the tic-tac-toe television game show. The brother of Joanne Dru, Marshall was born in Huntington, West Virginia.

◀ GEORGE BRETT

ATHLETES

George Brett (born 1953), a baseball player from Glen Dale, West Virginia, was named the American League's Most Valuable Player in 1980 for his high batting average. Brett retired in 1993 after 20 years with the Kansas City Royals.

Gino Marchetti (born 1927), elected to the Pro Football Hall of Fame in 1972, was born in Smithers, West Virginia. A defensive end for the Baltimore Colts, Marchetti played in 11 straight Pro Bowls and was named All-Pro seven times before retiring in 1966.

Mary Lou Retton (born 1968) is a gymnast who gained fame at the 1984 Olympics as the first American to win a gold medal in the women's all-around gymnastics competition. Winning three additional medals, the native of Fairmont, West Virginia, earned more awards than any other U.S. athlete at that year's games.

Jerry West (born 1938) grew up in Chelyan, West Virginia. A guard for the Los Angeles Lakers, West retired in 1974 with the fourth best career scoring average in the National Basketball Association's history. He has since become the Lakers' general manager.

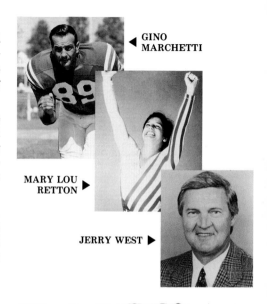

◀ GINO MARCHETTI

MARY LOU RETTON ▶

JERRY WEST ▶

◀ JOHNSON NEWLON CAMDEN

HENRY FORD SINCLAIR ▶

BUSINESS LEADERS

Johnson Newlon Camden (1828–1908), from Braxton County, West Virginia, helped develop the oil industry in West Virginia in the 1860s. Later, he organized the Ohio River Railroad and was president of the West Virginia and Pittsburgh Railroad.

Henry Ford Sinclair (1876–1953), born in Wheeling, West Virginia, founded the Sinclair Consolidated Oil Corporation in 1919 and built it into a multimillion dollar business. The corporation operated gas stations across the country and owned millions of acres of oil fields in many parts of the world.

63

Robert C. Byrd (born 1917) broadcast weekly sermons on the radio and ran a grocery store before entering politics in the 1940s. Raised in the coal-mining town of Stotesbury, West Virginia, Byrd has served in the U.S. Senate since 1959.

Thomas ("Stonewall") Jackson (1824–1863), born in Clarksburg, West Virginia, led Confederate troops to victory over Union forces in several major Civil War battles. The Confederate general earned his nickname because of the way he stood his ground "like a stone wall" at the First Battle of Bull Run in 1861.

Cyrus Vance (born 1917), a lawyer and diplomat from Clarksburg, West Virginia, was appointed U.S. secretary of state under President Jimmy Carter. From 1991 to 1993, Vance served as a United Nations representative, working to resolve the conflict in Bosnia-Herzegovina (formerly part of Yugoslavia).

▲ ROBERT C. BYRD

▲ STONEWALL JACKSON

◄ CYRUS VANCE

MUSICIANS

Phyllis Curtin (born 1927) first sang at the New York City Opera in 1959. A leading soprano, Curtin also sang at the Metropolitan Opera and performed with orchestras across the world. Curtin is from Clarksburg, West Virginia.

Bill Withers (born 1938), a singer and songwriter whose style combines funk, soul, and jazz, was born in Slab Fork, West Virginia. He has recorded several top hits, including "Ain't No Sunshine," "Lean on Me," and "Just the Two of Us"—a song that won a Grammy Award in 1982.

▲ PHYLLIS CURTIN

▲ BILL WITHERS

SOCIAL LEADERS

Tony Brown (born 1933) is the host of "Tony Brown's Journal," a television program that has explored social issues from an African American perspective for more than 20 years. Raised in Charleston, Brown founded the Howard University School of Communications in Washington, D.C., in 1971 to help blacks succeed in the communications field.

Walter Reuther (1907–1970), from Wheeling, West Virginia, was president of the United Automobile Workers union from 1946 until his death. The labor leader helped workers gain higher wages and better benefits.

▲ TONY BROWN

◄ WALTER REUTHER

◄ PEARL S. BUCK

WALTER DEAN ► MYERS

WRITERS

Pearl S. Buck (1892–1973) drew upon her experiences growing up in China to become an award-winning author. In 1932 she received a Pulitzer Prize for her most famous book, *The Good Earth.* Born in Hillsboro, West Virginia, Buck was awarded the Nobel Prize for literature in 1938.

John Knowles (born 1926) is a writer from Fairmont, West Virginia. His first and best-known novel, *A Separate Peace,* was published in 1960. Later works include *Indian Summer* and *Peace Breaks Out.*

Walter Dean Myers (born 1937), a native of Martinsburg, West Virginia, writes about the lives of young African Americans. Among his most famous children's books are *The Young Landlords* and *Motown and Didi: A Love Story,* both of which have won a Coretta Scott King Award.

Facts-at-a-Glance

Nickname: Mountain State
Songs: "The West Virginia Hills," "This Is My West Virginia," "West Virginia My Home Sweet Home"
Motto: *Montani Semper Liberi* (Mountaineers Are Always Free)
Flower: rhododendron
Tree: sugar maple
Bird: cardinal

Population: 1,793,477*
Rank in population, nationwide: 34th
Area: 24,231 sq mi (62,758 sq km)
Rank in area, nationwide: 41st
Date and ranking of statehood:
June 20, 1863, the 35th state
Capital: Charleston
Major cities (and populations*):
Charleston (57,287), Huntington (54,844), Wheeling (34,882), Parkersburg (33, 862), Morgantown (25,879)
U.S. senators: 2
U.S. representatives: 3
Electoral votes: 5

Places to visit: South Charleston Mound in South Charleston, Smoke Hole Caverns in Seneca Rocks, Huntington Museum of Art in Huntington, Blackwater Falls State Park near Davis, National Radio Astronomy Observatory in Green Bank

Annual events: Winterfest in Richwood (Feb.), State Jazz Festival in Charleston (March), Appalachian Weekend in Pipestem (March), Jamboree in the Hills in Wheeling (July), West Virginia State Fair in Fairlea (Aug.), Mountain State Forest Festival in Elkins (Oct.)

*1990 census

Natural resources: coal, natural gas, oil, brine, rock salt, limestone, sand, clay, dolomite, sandstone, shale, fertile soil

Agricultural products: beef cattle, milk, chickens, turkeys, hay, corn, tobacco, apples, peaches

Manufactured goods: dyes, detergents, paints, plastics, synthetic rubber, salt cake, tin plate, sheet and structural steel, nickel, glassware, pottery, pipes, tools, mining machinery, soft drinks, baked goods

ENDANGERED AND THREATENED SPECIES
Mammals—Virginia big-eared bat, Indiana bat, gray bat, northern flying squirrel, eastern cougar
Birds—peregrine falcon, bald eagle
Mollusks—pink mucket pearly mussel, ringpink, fanshell, clubshell, tuberculed-blossom pearly mussel, James spiny mussel, northern riffleshell, flat-spired three-toothed land snail
Amphibians—Cheat Mountain salamander
Plants—shale barren rockcress, running buffalo clover, harperella, northeastern bulrush, Virginia spiraea

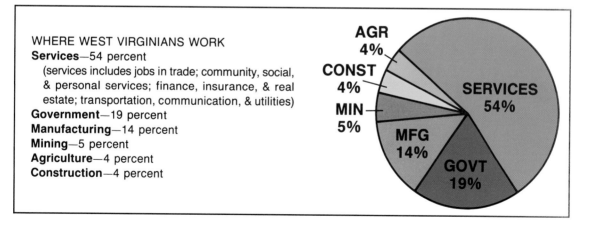

WHERE WEST VIRGINIANS WORK
Services—54 percent
(services includes jobs in trade; community, social, & personal services; finance, insurance, & real estate; transportation, communication, & utilities)
Government—19 percent
Manufacturing—14 percent
Mining—5 percent
Agriculture—4 percent
Construction—4 percent

AGR
4%
CONST
4%
MIN
5%
MFG
14%
GOVT
19%
SERVICES
54%

PRONUNCIATION GUIDE

Allegheny (al-uh-GAY-nee)

Appalachian (ap-uh-LAY-chuhn)

Cherokee (CHEHR-uh-kee)

Greenbrier (GREEN-bry-ur)

Iroquois (IHR-uh-kwoy)

Kanawha (kuh-NAW-wuh)

Mingo (MIHNG-goh)

Monongahela (muh-nahn-guh-HEE-luh)

Potomac (puh-TOH-mihk)

Seneca (SEHN-ih-kuh)

Shawnee (shaw-NEE)

Glossary

colony A territory ruled by a country some distance away.

constitution The system of basic laws or rules of a government, society, or organization. The document in which these laws or rules are written.

groundwater Water that lies beneath the earth's surface. The water comes from rain and snow that seep through soil into the cracks and other openings in rocks. Groundwater supplies wells and springs.

immigrant A person who moves into a foreign country and settles there.

landfill A place specially prepared for burying solid waste.

leachate Liquid that has seeped through waste or that forms when waste rots in a landfill. Leachate can contaminate water or soil.

plantation A large estate, usually in a warm climate, on which crops are grown by workers who live on the estate. In the past, plantation owners usually used slave labor.

plateau A large, relatively flat area that stands above the surrounding land.

precipitation Rain, snow, and other forms of moisture that fall to earth.

treaty An agreement between two or more groups, usually having to do with peace or trade.

Index ▰▰▰▰▰▰▰▰▰▰▰▰▰▰▰▰▰▰▰▰▰▰

Acknowledgments:

Maryland Cartographics, Inc., pp. 2, 10; Jerry Hennen, pp. 2-3, 9 (inset), 13, 15, 44, 68; Jack Lindstrom, p. 7; Frederica Georgia, pp. 6, 11; © Scott T. Smith, pp. 8-9, 17 (left), 41, 46, 50, 71; David Dvorak, Jr., pp. 13 (inset), 17 (right); WV Division of Tourism & Parks: David E. Fattaleh, pp. 14, 45 (bottom), Stephen J. Shaluta, Jr., pp. 20, 42, 49, 51 (right), 53 (inset), Larry Belcher, p. 51 (left); Conrad A. Gutraj / Root Resources, p. 16; © 1995 Charles Braswell, Jr., p. 17 (inset); © 1995 Penny Braswell, pp. 52-53; Smithsonian Institution, #80-1819, p. 18; Virginia State Library & Archives, pp. 21, 22, 25 (top), 28, 32; West Virginia State Archives, pp. 23, 24, 30, 35, 63 (top center and bottom left); Library of Congress, pp. 27, 33, 36, 38; Harpers Ferry National Historical Park, p. 29; WV & Regional History Collection, WV University Library, p. 34; Alexandria Library, Lloyd House, pp. 36-37; Lawrence Pierce, *Charleston Gazette*, p. 39; *Dictionary of American Portraits*, p. 25 (bottom); © 1995 Thomas R. Fletcher, p. 43; © W. Lynn Seldon, Jr., pp. 45 (top), 54; Robert E. Cramer / Geographical Slides, pp. 46-47; Barbara L. Moore / NE Stock Photo, p. 48; WV Solid Waste Management Board, p. 55; Tony LaGruth, p. 56; Jim West / Impact Visuals, p. 57; WV Division of Natural Resources, pp. 59, 61; Hollywood Book & Poster, p. 62 (top right and left); Kansas City Royals, p. 62 (bottom); Baltimore Colts, p. 63 (top left); Los Angeles Lakers, p. 63 (top right); American Heritage Center, University of Wyoming, p. 63 (bottom right); U.S. Signal Corps, National Archives, p. 64 (top center); Metropolitan Opera Archives, p. 64 (bottom left); Todd Grey, p. 64 (bottom right); Tony Brown Productions, Inc., p. 65 (top right); Independent Picture Service, p. 65 (top left); Pearl S. Buck, p. 65 (bottom left); Ken Petretti, p. 65 (bottom right); Jean Matheny, p. 66.